THE ATOMIC INNOVATION HANDBOOK

HOW TO ENABLE A SUSTAINABLE CULTURE OF INNOVATION

SCOTT WILLIAMS

TEN PERCENT

For Anne, Christian and Kyle

CONTENTS

INTRODUCTION

Innovation is a topic most organisations talk about at one time or another. Bloggers write about it, consultants develop strategies around it, and coaches help teams adopt new techniques to deliver it. Labs are created, fancy titles are bestowed, and transformations are undertaken in an attempt to be seen as leaders in it. Maybe you've heard someone in your own company say something like this: "Our new innovation strategy will allow us to better meet the expectations of our customers now and into the future." Or perhaps you've read an article that claims: "Leaders must create a culture of innovation to compete in the modern business world."

There are some flaws in those statements. Leaders don't actually create a culture; they can only support the behaviours and interactions that allow it to emerge. Also, it's not your strategy that will allow you to better meet customer expectations, but instead your practical ability to deliver against that strategy. Still, recognising that something must be done is a good first step. Now it's time to talk seriously about taking the next one. That is the purpose of this book.

It's likely that your company has experienced an increase in customer appetite and expectation for change. Drivers of customer loyalty are shifting from price and quality to overall experience[1]. If we aren't constantly focused on solving important problems and improving key experiences for our customers, we can be quickly surpassed by a competitor who is - and we may not ever see it coming.

Many businesses also realise that the discussion around innovation must extend beyond products and services if they are to truly succeed in achieving their goals. Intuit expects 43% of their workforce to be gig-economy workers by 2020[2], which means less full-time positions in favour of more short-term, independent contracts. In response, organisations will need to innovate their structural and operational models to attract and retain top talent.

Culture is important, too. Findings from PwC's 2017 Innovation Benchmark report[3] indicate that the key factors when talking about innovation are human ones. In it, 65% of respondents said behaviours and culture are the most important aspects of successful innovation. This tells us that a large part of our energy should be dedicated to understanding the behaviours that support this success, and to figuring out a way to make sure they are exhibited in everything we do.

Before we get into the detail of what to do about all of this, let's review a couple of key concepts.

Culture: *A set of attitudes, values and practices shared by a particular group of people.*

Fortunately for us, culture is emergent. It's fortunate because rather than being something that simply pops into existence without clear explanation, culture is the result of more basic components evolving over time. By putting our effort into understanding and supporting those components, we can use the knowledge to manipulate them in a way that encourages the attitudes, values and practices we recognise in innovative business cultures.

We can't think that innovation will happen after we have created a particular culture, because the reverse is true. Only when innovation becomes an inevitable output of everyday work throughout our organisations will we have the right to proclaim ourselves as having the corresponding culture.

Innovation: *Solving problems in ways they haven't been solved before, by using solutions in ways they've never been used before, to create experiences that are better than they've ever been before.*

Just as we don't "implement" a culture, we also don't "do" innovation. Innovation is the output we get from the behaviours of, and interactions between, colleagues and partners. It's these behaviours and interactions that we need to comprehend at the most fundamental level if we are to identify solutions and design experiences that our customers will consider innovative.

In this book, we will explore what I call Atomic Innovation. It's a model describing the underlying characteristics that drive tangible innovation, ultimately enabling a sustainable innovative culture to emerge. We will talk practically about turning words and definitions into actions and measures, and how those components relate to each other in a holistic approach to achieving our innovation goals.

PART I

1

THE INNOVATION ATOM

Why atomic? Isn't it crazy to describe one difficult thing (innovation) by comparing it to something even more difficult (atomic physics)? Surely there has to be something more familiar to the daily human experience we can use instead, right?

Have no fear. It's the structure of atoms and their subatomic constituents – not the function – that I'm using as an analogy here. It's this structure that perfectly describes how we can bring together and make use of the fundamental characteristics that drive innovation.

Let me explain how.

Scientists have long known that every atom of regular matter in the universe is actually the output of more fundamental interactions. The strong force binds quarks together to form the protons and neutrons that make up the nucleus, which is surrounded by a cloud of probability we call electrons[4].

While there are different ways of arranging these components, there is only one way to arrange them to get a particular element with specific properties. If you don't have two Up quarks and one Down quark, you can't make a proton. If you want Helium, you must use exactly two protons. Add or remove a proton and you will get something, but it won't be Helium. The specificity of the formula means accurate predictions can be made about the output of a particular quantity and arrangement of subatomic particles.

Just like an atom, what we experience as innovation is simply the output observed and measured resulting from a more fundamental set of characteristics. Similarly, if we don't put these characteristics together in the right way, and in the right amount, we won't get the innovation we are after. Through some clever operational alchemy, we can make accurate predictions about the level of innovation that will emerge from our organisations. It will become an inevitable consequence of our everyday work even when we aren't trying, to the benefit of our business, our colleagues and our customers.

As with all analogies, it's not perfect. Thinking about it this way, however, helps create a picture of how all the necessary pieces fit together.

So, what is the structure of an Atomic Innovation atom? We will need:

A **Vision Proton**. A clear vision gives us direction and defines what we are ultimately trying to achieve. To produce a Vision Proton, we bring together three behavioural quarks: the Curiosity, Creativity and Imagination that it takes to create a vision of the future worth pursuing. Binding these quarks together is the Courage it takes to allow these behaviours to manifest in our approach to work.

A **Collaboration Neutron**. The best outcomes arise when we work together with people from different backgrounds and make decisions informed by people with different viewpoints. To create this Collaboration Neutron, we leverage the same Courage to bring together three interaction quarks: the Communication, Transparency and Trust necessary to work with others effectively.

An **Entrepreneurship Electron**. For our innovation

atom to be complete, we need to include the ability to turn our vision into something tangible. This is where an Entrepreneurship Electron comes in. Kept in place around the nucleus by the Excitement of doing something new, this particle creates the shell of delivery that makes an innovation atom something we can observe and measure.

That's all there is to it. No matter the size of your organisation, the goal is always the same: fill your operational space with as many innovation atoms as you can. Scaling the model to produce innovation of increasing complexity is done simply by adding more Vision Protons, Collaboration Neutrons and Entrepreneurship Electrons to the mix. In fact, rather than "scaling" the model, we should think about it as a way to de-scale the organisation, making it easier for more people to exhibit the behaviours and experience the interactions in their day-to-day work.

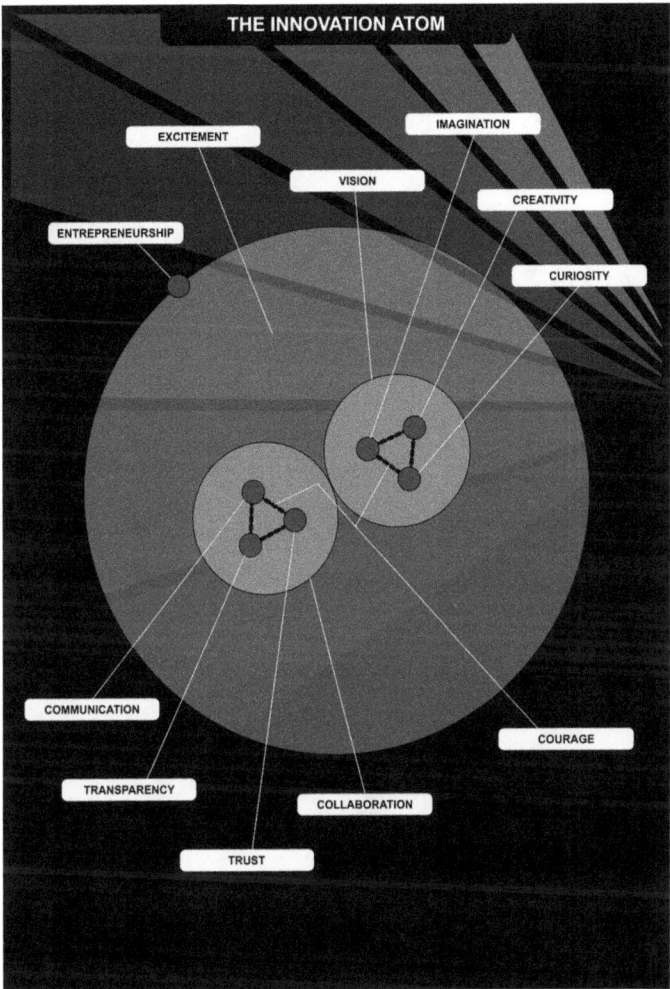

THE INNOVATION ATOM

PART II

2

VISION PROTON

If we are innovating, that means we are doing work. It takes a lot of work to solve problems in new ways. In some businesses, that could mean you've been tasked with delivering a particular project. If your organisation is more Design Thinking savvy, then the work is likely framed as being entrusted to solve an important customer problem. Regardless of how you describe it, the first thing people typically ask is "what's your plan?" They want to know how you are going to get from point A to point B[5].

Before you can create a plan, however, you need a strategy: the "what" you are going to do (and not do) to reach point B. So, to create a plan, you need a strategy. To create a strategy, you need a clear description of the point B you are trying to reach. You need a vision.

Vision: *A description of what could be in the future.*

If you are a follower of The Lean Startup[6], you know that establishing a clear vision at the beginning of any piece of work is one of the most important things you can do[7]. It doesn't matter whether you are starting a new business, leading a project, or working as a member of a modern delivery team. Understanding what you want the future to be like helps determine what work is most important, and what work can wait or be completely ignored.

That future, by the way, should be long-term. A good vision is not a short-term objective or a specific project milestone. It's also not the implementation of a particular system or use of a certain type of tool. Think of your vision as the description of a desired future-state which tells others what the world will be like when you get there.

Ultimately, a vision is the determining factor in what is perceived as success or failure, and helps everyone answer the following question: "Are we still headed in the right direction?" If the answer is no, or you can't clearly explain how then it's time to re-evaluate what you are doing. It's the one thing that remains constant, even when your strategy and plans change.

Let's take a look at some real-world examples:

<u>Amazon</u>: "Our vision is to be the earth's most customer-centric company; to build a place where people can come to find and discover anything they might want to buy online."[8]

<u>Caterpillar</u>: "Our vision is a world in which all people's basic needs — such as shelter, clean water, sanitation, food and reliable power — are fulfilled in an environmentally sustainable way and a company that improves the quality of the environment and the communities where we live and work."[9]

Sure; those examples are business-level vision statements, but what if you are creating a new product or service? Consider this one:

<u>Amazon Kindle</u>: "To make available in less than 60 seconds every book, ever written, in any language, in print or out of print; and bring the same ease-of-use, deep integration and superior selection of content to movies, TV shows, music, magazines, apps, games, and more."[10]

No matter what you are doing, whether it's a small improvement to how you perform your job, or creating an entirely new business unit, having a clear vision of the future will help everyone keep their activities aligned to the desired end result.

Visions are intensely personal things. They don't often translate well from one setting to another because the context is always different. It's important to allow people who are working together to use their collective curiosity, creativity and imagination to create a vision purpose-built for the task at hand. That's what we do when applying the Atomic Innovation model. Instead of focusing on the vision itself, we focus on the underlying behaviours that drive us towards creating a vision of the future worth the effort to achieve it.

We don't need everyone to be an expert in exhibiting these behaviours in order to get started. Using this model, we will introduce techniques and set up objective measures that indicate if they are present in our everyday work, whether we know it or not. By doing so, we drive towards innovative outputs as a natural result of how we do things.

3

CURIOSITY QUARK

VISION PROTON

Curiosity: *A strong desire to learn and understand.*

The best ways of doing work in a modern company are design-led. The mindset, methods and techniques that make up a designers toolkit are purposefully crafted to take a concept or idea from thought-bubble to reality along the best possible path. One of the main reasons for this is that design-led approaches are inherently curious. The customer-centric focus on empathy and insight, even when the "customer" is internal to the organisation, ensures that we are doing the right things for the right people.

When you start to boost your design capability, a recurring pattern will begin to emerge. Every conversation, in every meeting, and around every wall of sticky notes, will start with "What problem are we trying to solve here?" As frustrating as it will feel in the beginning, it's exactly what needs to happen. If we want to have any chance of producing a valuable output through a piece of work, we must begin by getting to the bottom of what's wrong with the way things are now.

According to some contemporary scientific views, curiosity is a special form of internally motivated information-seeking[11]. In everyday language, however, we can think about it as our drive to know things we didn't know before. At work, we need to encourage people to learn as much as possible to understand any problem we are trying to solve. In fact, it's curiosity that helps us gather the necessary information to identify the problems worth solving in the first place. "What else can we learn about the problems faced by our business and our customers?" "What underlying factors are causing those problems?" "Who cares if we solve them, and why is it so important?" These are the types of critical questions we begin to ask ourselves when we are curious.

In Atomic Innovation, we don't sit back and hope that people will be curious. We develop methods and practices to set ourselves up in a way so that it becomes an innate part of how we do things, even if that is not our default state of mind at the time. We look for practical things we can do to draw out curiosity amongst our people and make it a part of their daily work.

The most effective thing we can do is change how we measure performance and reward people. It's most effective because there aren't many methods of drawing out particular behaviours in the workplace more potent than recognition and compensation. When times get tough and deadlines are looming, people will prioritise those things that have the potential to help or harm their reputation with colleagues, the outcome of their next performance review, or their chance to receive financial compensation that might be subject to a particular result.

———

If you find yourself in a leadership position where people report progress of work to you, ask them a different set of questions. Instead of "How have things progressed since we last met?", ask "What have you learned since the last time we met?" Don't let them off the hook. Make it clear that the most important thing you want to know is what new knowledge about their customer, their solution, or the broader work landscape they have obtained. Ask them if the new knowledge they've uncovered should cause a change in the work, and if so, what they are going to do about it. If they have not set themselves up to execute in this way, help them change their approach so that they are testing assumptions and gathering new data in small chunks, more quickly.

Change the way you report the status of work to other stakeholders, as well. For example, if you use a standard Red / Amber / Green system for communicating status, re-define what those colours mean. Red will no longer mean behind schedule or lack of resources. Now it means we have failed to learn anything new and therefore are making too many risky guesses.

The point here is to make the people reporting to you accountable for gaining new knowledge and information – to learn - and to measure their performance based on that accountability.

———

Introduce a mandate that each person will submit one idea for improving something about their role on a regular basis, perhaps every 3 months. It doesn't matter what it is, as long as it's something about their job that has the potential to be improved upon. By adding this as a defined job responsibility, you are forcing them to learn more about what they do in greater detail than they might have otherwise, and to think about how it could be better. Create a central location where these ideas are submitted in a way that allows everyone else to see them: a wall with manually-written cards on it, a digital tool everyone can access - whatever is appropriate for your situation. Hold regular sessions with all your people to talk through these ideas, share information, and discuss what might be done with them.

To support this, your organisation must allow each person to take the time necessary to adhere to this new responsibility. Even if it's only 1 hour per week, make it clear that this is not a request or an opportunity - it's a requirement.

As mentioned in a previous chapter, innovation is about more than just products and services. By introducing this type of system, we not only force an increased level of curiosity about our own jobs, but we also start to work towards innovating how we operate as a business.

———

If some of your people are put together to form teams to deliver specific projects, how are those people selected? If it's not already, include a person's interest in the topic or problem space to the key criteria used when assigning them to a team. The more motivated someone is about a particular topic, the more they learn and the more curious they will become[12]. This means if we can better align people to their interests, we get the curiosity we are after with little to no extra effort. It's well known in startup circles that the best companies are founded by people who are knowledgeable and passionate about a specific problem[13]. This applies to the non-startup world as well, where the best projects are run by people with the same level of knowledge and passion about the outcome they are trying to achieve.

If your organisation is courageous enough, set up a process where people can choose for themselves the projects they want to work on. Before you say anything, I'm not talking about traditional secondment processes here. Those typically have too much overhead and management noise associated with them. Using a system that everyone can access, post the projects that need to be done and the roles required to deliver them. Give everyone a chance to volunteer for those roles regardless of their title or position. For the duration of that project, that is their new job. Not only are you creating personal and professional development opportunities for your people, but they will be more motivated to do the right things because of their self-selected passion for the work.

Even if your business isn't ready to go quite that far, at least talk to your people and understand where their passions lie. Consider this when distributing them to teams, because what gets delivered will benefit from their natural curiosity.

———

For some people, being curious is a natural state. But even if others are simply motivated by the measures you put in place that affect their personal gain, it's worth it. This is ultimately about pulling together a worthwhile vision, which starts with a curiosity for learning about the most important problems faced by our customers and understanding why they want them solved.

4

CREATIVITY QUARK

VISION PROTON

Creativity: *Actively looking for ways to do things differently.*

If you haven't said it yourself, you've probably heard a colleague say, "I'm not creative." Typically, this is because they associate creativity with some sort of artistic ability or craft[14]. While those things do elicit observations of creativity, that's all they are: observations. If you think about it, we don't often look at our own work and claim it to be creative. That determination comes from others who review what we've done and describe it as being so.

What really matters is if our customer, whether internal or external, considers what we are doing creative. In 2017, results of a study published on the Harvard Business Review website found 10 common creativity cues that were agreed upon by both Chinese and American consumers[15]. Among these cues were things that represented a significant change in thinking, the ability to do things others failed to do, and an integration of function and features that were distinct. The commonalities uncovered support the idea that a description of creativity is ultimately determined by something being different than what has been experienced before.

In the Atomic Innovation model, we encourage creativity by taking time to identify and implement those differences. This could be a process internal to your organisation, a service provided to operational partners, or a product offered to customers. Whatever the scenario, it will be time well spent when you have identified that one critical thing that better solves an important problem or greatly improves a customer experience.

To support the expectation that everyone will put effort into doing things differently, the organisation must be willing to change the way it operates to allow people the freedom to work towards that goal.

———

Set a general policy that when launching a new product or service, you won't simply duplicate what competitors are already doing. These are often called "me too" products. Communicate that policy to everyone so that no pitch, canvas or business case gets submitted proposing such a thing. It may seem too obvious a step, but it's an easy place to start.

Before you do any piece of work, make it a requirement that all the ways that customers solve a particular problem today get identified. This is more than just creating a list of who you think the competitors are. The list may also include some combination of other methods that customers have come up with on their own. The only way to know for sure is to engage your customers directly and find out. Once you have that list, design your solution so that isn't an exact copy of any. The differences don't necessarily need to be massive, but they do need to be clear and important. When we put a new product in market, we are asking customers to stop doing one thing and to do another. To make such a suggestion, the benefits to those customers must be worth the effort it takes to change.

Don't think of duplicating what already exists as the only option for getting to market quickly. We definitely want to get things into the hands of our customers as soon as possible, but that doesn't mean we have to copy what already exists in order to get there. In fact, rapidly testing our key differentiators in market will tell us much more quickly, and with much more confidence, if we are headed in the right direction.

Adopting this type of policy guides people towards doing things differently, producing outputs that could be described as creative, and therefore potentially innovative.

———

To get things done in your organisation, how is funding requested and approved? What determines how long something will take? Often, a group of experts is brought together to create some sort of estimate. Depending on how many times the experts have done that exact thing, with those exact tools, and in that exact context, the estimates will range in accuracy from "we think we're pretty close" to "we have no idea, so we took a guess and doubled it."

Stop asking people how much money will be needed to do something, or how long they think it will take. Instead, tell them how much they have to spend, and how long they have to do it. The trade off: you will have to change what is meant by the "it" people are asked to "do". In this approach, the goal becomes solving an identified problem or achieving a particular outcome in any way possible within the set constraints. You'll need to shift away from a project mindset, where discrete pieces of work have a defined start and end to produce a pre-determined output. In its place, adopt an experimental mindset and iterative delivery approach where concepts evolve over time, and investment continues indefinitely in small chunks as long as there is continued evidence to support it.

How do you determine these constraints? One way to think about it is this: How much time and money are you willing to spend in order to learn if it's worth spending any more? Early in the concept development process, your confidence in an idea being the right thing to do will be low, but it will increase as you gain more information. Therefore, align your commitment to match your confidence level at that time and allocate resources accordingly. Start with small budgets and short time frames to test your riskiest assumptions. As you learn more and confidence in your ability to deliver against the long-term vision increases, your commitment of time and money can grow along with it.

Remember that what we are trying to do is drive people towards creative outputs, even if they themselves don't recognise the creativity while they are doing it. The introduction of sensible constraints is a positive way to guide people towards seeking out different ways of delivering the outcome they are tasked to achieve.

————

Measure employees by the number of experiments they run regarding how their own job is done. This moves us beyond the simple suggestion of improvement opportunities we discussed in the chapter on Curiosity and gets people to run the actual experiments themselves. Set a minimum per year and introduce that as a requirement of their role. I'm going to call out the obvious exemption here for those jobs where the consequence of experimentation is measured in life and death: medical doctors, veterinarians, etc. Having acknowledged that, however, the more we test ways of doing our job differently, the better chance we have of doing our job better.

Make any necessary changes to your organisational and operational structures so that any group of people can work together to test different ways of doing their jobs without needing formal approval from a higher authority. If they have to request permission from various managers to run every small experiment, that overhead will end up making people's work lives more difficult. Establish a centralised system where all experiments are published so that everyone can see what's going on. This will keep those managers informed, while discouraging people from trying to game the system by running bad experiments simply to meet a quota.

You may choose to require more formal approval before making a permanent change if the result of an experiment indicates a better way of working, especially if it's one that affects people not directly involved with the experiment itself. There's nothing wrong with coordinating effective change across your organisation. Do make it mandatory, however, that anyone who opposes the change produce evidence or data to support their claim that things should stay the same.

———

Creativity does not mean introducing complexity. One of my favourite science communicators, Neil DeGrasse Tyson, has said: "If I had to give you a complex theory to understand a complex phenomenon, you know, send me home."[16] For those of us that need to apply that way of thinking in a business setting, I think this means that we shouldn't accept proposals to do something complex unless we are confident that all best efforts have been made to simplify it. It also means we should guard against the desire to design complex solutions just to show off our ability to do something complex. Sure, it could impress the random colleague or boss, but doing so puts us on the wrong path. It's much more creative to find simple ways to solve complex problems than it is to implement solutions just as complex.

So far, we have leveraged our curiosity to understand why things should change, and now our creativity has been used to find different ways of implementing that change. We're gathering the necessary components to assemble our Vision Proton, which advances us in our journey towards creating a view of the future worthy of the time and effort it will take to reach it.

5

IMAGINATION QUARK

VISION PROTON

Imagination: *Seeking out that which is not currently obvious to the senses.*

It appears there's no evidence that Henry Ford ever said the words "If I had asked people what they wanted, they would have said faster horses."[17] Someone, however, did write or say those words at some point. They are often quoted when talking about innovation as a way of claiming that customers don't know what they want.

One-third of that claim is wrong. Customers know what problems they experience and can tell you which ones of those problems they wish someone would solve. In that sense, they know exactly what they want. It's why a key and critical part of modern concept development practices are based on talking to customers directly as a method of understanding their needs before we do anything else.

Two-thirds of the claim is correct. It's not always obvious to customers that the problem they experience is actually caused by something else, nor are all the potential ways the problem could be solved. The same is true for the people in our organisations who are entrusted to try and solve these problems. When faced with a scenario, we use our senses to evaluate the situation and then draw upon our experience to respond quickly in a way that we think is best. This seems to be a trait shared by everyone that naturally comes out as our default approach to work, and it's a useful one for getting us started.

Unfortunately, this trait alone won't get us to the level of innovation we need for the corresponding culture to emerge. For that to happen, we need to go beyond our basic instincts by using data and insights to find the problems that aren't obvious to our senses. We then need to put effort into searching for ways to solve problems that not only extend beyond our own experiences, but sometimes fly directly in the face of them. Experience is always based on the past, and therefore cannot possibly represent all possible future paths with any certainty.

Talking about imagination in the workplace can at first seem a little fluffy. However, there are ways of working we can put in place so that imagination, as defined by the Atomic Innovation model, becomes something we can expect and measure.

———

Teach everyone in your organisation how to use contemporary techniques for customer insight gathering and synthesis when approaching any piece of work. I'm not only talking about the people developing new consumer-facing products and services, but also those simply trying to do their job a bit better. Bring in experts who already know how to use methods such as Jobs To Be Done[18], Five Why's[19], or others and have them work alongside your people until they learn to do it themselves.

If you find yourself as a stakeholder for work and receive status updates, ask for a high-level description of the methods used to gather customer insights and how the people doing the work used this knowledge when deciding what to do next. Request a visual representation that summarises how these learnings compare to the outcomes they are trying to achieve. When people are first learning how to use these techniques, it would be a good idea to make sure this goes beyond a bullet point in a document presented at some sort of committee meeting so that no one can pretend to have done it when they haven't.

Not everyone is naturally a maverick who loves charging into the unknown. Many people in the workplace want a process to follow or tool to use when being asked to do something they've never done before. By teaching and supporting these types of tools and methods, we can help our people identify the less obvious problems and solutions.

———

When designing solutions, ask people to clearly articulate what they are trying to achieve, and then figure out what it would take to ensure the exact opposite occurs. Have them think about how all the pieces would fit together to make that happen, and roughly visualise how it would work from beginning to end. This is a useful exercise because it can help uncover things you hadn't thought of before. Causes of potential weakness in design can become obvious when they may not have been previously.

What you end up with through this type of approach is a blueprint for what not to do. At a minimum, it can help identify major threats to a successful delivery of customer and business value.

As with the other techniques discussed in this book, it's not enough to simply ask people to do these kinds of things. Atomic Innovation requires us to implement methods of measurement to ensure they are happening. So, make it a requirement that whenever a new solution is proposed, the team proposing it demonstrate what a solution would look like to make the opposite outcome happen. Make them walk you through that solution, talking about what the customer journey would be like, and what they've learned because of it.

This type of exercise doesn't add a lot of time to the solution design process, but it does help uncover knowledge that could have remained hidden.

———

Co-create with people from different parts of your business, and whenever possible, external parties. For those businesses that have adopted design-led approaches to problem-solving, this is probably already happening at some level. If it isn't, then set an expectation that it will happen, every time.

Whatever your governance process is for selecting and prioritising work, make this a key part of the criteria used when deciding what work to fund. As a starting point, require that at least one person from another part of the business be involved in the early ideation process for each problem you want to solve. This means that each person in the organisation will need to set aside some percentage of their working time to participate in these types of activities, but it doesn't have to be a lot. Attendance at a single brainstorming workshop, or participation in another team's regular working group sessions, is a step in the right direction towards leveraging the knowledge and expertise of others not historically engaged.

Where possible, invite partners or other external parties to participate in the process. Make them part of the team. Ask them if they have ever faced similar problems, and how they solved them, even if the context was completely different. The act of exploring ways to take a solution from one space and apply it to another can get people thinking about alternative possibilities that were not previously considered. Sometimes you will find that, with perhaps a few tweaks, you could partner with the external party involved to deliver something unique for you both, which would be a big win for everyone. If you are worried about intellectual property, you can come to some basic agreement in advance. Don't worry about it too much, though. The benefits that arise from this level of collaboration will far outweigh any perceived loss of value by sharing ideas with others.

A mandate to include outsiders in the ideation process can be the quickest way to identify things not immediately obvious to those already involved.

———

We now have an understanding of the fundamental components that make up our Vision Proton. We've discussed giving our people the opportunity to use their collective curiosity, creativity and imagination. By making use of some personal and professional courage, which we will discuss in a later chapter, we can bind these components together in a meaningful way that produces that vision.

It will take a working environment conducive to such behaviours, with responsibility for creating that environment falling squarely on the shoulders of leaders within the business. Keep this responsibility in mind as you experiment with your own ways of enabling, enhancing, and sometimes forcing these behaviours in the day-to-day work of everyone.

PART III

6

COLLABORATION NEUTRON

Depending on the type of work that you do, it's likely that at some point you will be required to collaborate with at least one other person to deliver it. It could be within your own team, as part of a group put together for a particular piece of work, or more broadly with those across your organisation or partner networks. No matter the scale, the ability to interact effectively with other people can be a major determining factor in whether the vision for that work is eventually realised.

Think back to the times where you were asked to do something and needed to work with someone else to get it done. Consider whether you collaborated well, and how that impacted the outcome. In the majority of project reviews or retrospectives I've been in where things could have gone better, the interactions between different people and groups were included in the list of reasons.

Collaboration: *Two or more people working together to produce an outcome.*

There's a key difference between collaboration and cooperation, and we are after the former. To cooperate is essentially to play nice; to provide or share something that helps someone else do what they need to do. That something could be information, people, access to tools, or anything that enables them to get their job done. Collaboration, on the other hand, is the alignment of priorities and workloads that need to happen for people to put joint effort into achieving common goals[20].

Good collaboration takes effort and requires that everyone involved be present mentally, if not physically[21]. You're making a commitment to the people you are working with and asking for one in return. What each side gets in exchange for that commitment is access to the talents and expertise of all the others that enable better, more informed decision-making and better outcomes.

We must avoid thinking of collaboration as a way to make up for some sort of weakness or lack of ability associated with the people doing the work. Collaboration, in all its various forms, should be about enhancing and expanding existing capability to reach outcomes better than could be achieved without it. If you are a proponent of Lean management principles, as I am, you will know that growing leaders is one of them[22]. As we put this principle into practice, the leaders we are growing need to understand that we collaborate for the sake of the gains alone, and not because of any particular pains. They must embrace the benefits of good collaboration, and when they have the opportunity to enable it among colleagues and partners, they must use that opportunity to constantly and consistently push that message.

There are smaller things individuals can do to help spread that message as well. The next time you are asked to cooperate, what if you offered to collaborate? You won't be able to do this all the time but think about how you would convince the other person that you want to not only provide them with what they need, but to work with them to achieve their goal, and why you think the outcome will benefit. The better people are at convincing others of the value of good collaboration, the more they understand it themselves.

Even though collaboration can be hard, it's important and necessary. Sure, there are instances where you will work completely on your own and produce something that a colleague or customer considers innovative. But, would it have been better if you had collaborated with someone else? Strong collaboration with the right people creates visions that are bolder, solutions that are more unique, and outputs that are far more innovative than they would have been otherwise.

7

COMMUNICATION QUARK

COLLABORATION NEUTRON

Communication: *The two-way exchange of information and meaning.*

Once a piece of work has commenced, a common issue that can arise is communication[23]. No matter where you are in the delivery process, from the earliest stages of ideation through to ongoing operations, a decrease in effective communication between people and their stakeholders can have a negative impact on team stress levels and morale. You've likely seen it as much as I have. Word filters back to a team that someone doesn't think they are communicating well. The people in the team get angry, spend some amount of time telling each other why they are in fact communicating well, and rhetorically asking themselves what else people could possibly want. Tension levels rise, and then someone in the team sends out a ridiculously long email to stakeholders to "address a concern raised around the lack of communication."

We need to think of communication as more than a one-way street. In addition to the spreading of information to others, we must consider the responsibilities in this exchange of the ones for whom the information is intended. Perhaps you've heard this said by one colleague about another: "They need to work on their communication skills." It's possible that the person making that statement has forgotten the other side of the coin: being an active listener. The first response by anyone to a thought like "They aren't communicating well" should therefore be "Am I listening as well as I could be?" Stakeholders need to play their part in all of this by listening more than they speak, and by giving their full attention to the task of understanding the information that is being shared[24].

Good communication is also more than words, whether written or spoken. Your body language, eye contact, hand gestures, and tone all colour the message you are trying to convey[25]. In addition, these same physical cues are useful in determining in real-time if your message is resonating. You can usually tell by a simple nod of the head, or by a confused-looking glance towards another person, if you are getting your point across in a meaningful way. Using these non-verbal forms of communication in combination with your own natural language creates a total package of information that tells a story more easily consumed and understood by others.

Just as with the behaviours that make up a good vision, we should put in place expectations, policies and measures that force the interactions necessary for good communication so that they occur even when our people aren't aware they are using them.

———

Replace written progress status report documents with a live event where key stakeholders visit, either physically or virtually, the place where the team is actually doing the work. This forces people to listen to a complete message rather than just looking for the colour at the top of a report that's in their email inbox, and skimming quickly through the comments only when it's red. It also gives the person doing the reporting a broader range of physical communication techniques that can lend weight and clarity to the message.

If you are an organisation where the same groups of stakeholders need to be across many different things at once, attending a bunch of in-person sessions may not be practically possible or sustainable. If that's the case, consider recording your progress updates on video and publishing them for consumption at a time convenient to those with whom you are communicating. These videos don't need to be of high production quality or require expensive equipment to produce. The smartphone in the pockets of most of your teammates will do just fine. Record your live update as you would if the stakeholders were present and post them in a place easily accessed inside or outside of your office.

It's still good practice to have a centralised location where everyone in the organisation can review high-level information about what's been happening with any piece of work. This speaks to transparency, which we cover in the next chapter. Make it clear, however, that this is a backup system and not the primary method of communication with key stakeholders and other interested parties. If they want to really know what's going on, they need to consume the total message as it is intended through these in-person or recorded sessions.

A quick internet search will return many lists that describe differing views on the traits of great leaders. To me, there are two traits that are more important than any others: 1) Great leaders make their people feel empowered to trying new things, and 2) Great leaders make sure their teams know everything that's going on around them. As a leader, making these a priority will mean your people will make better decisions, and will not waste time pursuing work that does not support what the organisation is trying to achieve.

Train your leaders to share updated information about your business with their people and teams regularly. Make it a clear part of the job description that, as a leader, one of the primary responsibilities is to seek out information amongst their peers and share that back with their people in a timely manner. Create a mandate that these leaders hold regular sessions to relay new information while it's still current. Depending on the size of the group they lead, this could be accomplished in a variety of ways ranging from a weekly team meeting to a quarterly town hall. Measure the adherence of leaders to this mandate and include the result as a key part of evaluating their leadership effectiveness.

If everyone we work with feels comfortable attempting things that are different without fear of reprimand for failure, then we have created a path to more innovative outputs. That path, however, could lead us astray if our people don't understand our strategy or have the context of all that's going on around them. A commitment from leaders to provide that understanding and context means the innovative outputs our people create are aligned with where the organisation wants to go.

———

Give your people and teams more autonomy in what they do and how they do it. This may seem in opposition to the interaction being advocated in this chapter, but it's not actually about communicating less. While this approach may result in a reduction in the level of detail communicated, it should in no way be considered a suggestion to reduce the level of quality. Teams still need to be on the hook for effectively communicating progress towards an outcome to everyone who is interested.

It's the "progress towards an outcome" part that is crucial here. Remove any real or perceived obligation that people will communicate dynamic and fluid plans outside of the team who are actually doing the work. It's the team who are responsible for delivering a solution that solves the customer problems identified. They are the ones accountable to the organisation to do it in a way that delivers the expected business benefit, or to speak up immediately if either of those things no longer seem possible within the constraints imposed upon them. There's no reason that teams should waste time figuring out how to effectively communicate all the content necessary for outsiders to be able to comprehend every little detail.

By focusing on communicating progress at the outcome level, the people doing the work can devote less time to playing with words, and more time getting things done. It will also make the messages sent to stakeholders more clear, concise and relevant to what they actually need to know in order to pass on the message to others.

––––––

It is possible to over-communicate, so be on the lookout for that as well because doing so can wear out your audience. Good communication does not mean constantly bombarding your stakeholders with more information, and with more detail, than necessary. There is no way to determine in advance what the right frequency or level of detail will be because it all depends on what you are doing and who are you communicating with. Ask your key stakeholders what they expect, tell them what you're willing to do, and negotiate a level of communication in advance to avoid any issues down the track. To help people get started in that negotiation, decide what good communication looks like in your organisation, and then tell everyone so they can adjust their methods and content to match.

In the Atomic Innovation model, we get more innovative outputs by collaborating with others to do things differently. We start to make good collaboration a reality by ensuring quality communication is a part of our day-to-day interactions with colleagues and the broader organisation.

8

TRANSPARENCY QUARK

COLLABORATION NEUTRON

Transparency: *Full disclosure without hidden agendas or conditions.*

Have you ever felt the need to be guarded about what information to share, and what not to share, within your organisation? Perhaps it's a job-protection thing, or you're not sure of the consequences of sharing something that isn't a complete thought or polished output. What about the company itself? Does it ever seem like they are purposefully keeping people in the dark about the bigger picture, or telling an incomplete story about what's going on?

A serious commitment to transparency needs to be adopted and supported at all levels if we are to protect ourselves against these types of problems. The uncertainty and rumour associated with them can cause a negative hit to productivity and will directly limit the level of innovation going on within the company. In addition, it takes more effort to hide information or massage it into something that is a tailored representation of the truth. It's easier to make the raw truth available to everyone and keep the energy focused on what could be much more rewarding efforts.

Millennials, those born between 1980 and 2000, value visibility into decision-making processes and in finding ways to meaningfully contribute[26]. This means that as the world completes the transition in the next few years to this generational-majority workforce, transparency is only going to increase in its importance. If we want to be the place where top talent wants to work, we need to be as open and honest with them as we can be. Take Atlassian, for example, who has as one of their core company values: "Open company, no bullshit"[27]. The company website provides some context around this value which includes, in part, the statement that "information is open internally by default and sharing is a first principle." I believe that this is one of the reasons they are regularly rated by various sources as being among the best places to work.

By actively demonstrating an organisational dedication to transparency, we can help make our people feel comfortable doing the same. The level of innovation we are trying to achieve will only be possible if everyone feels completely safe in sharing information without fear of damage to their reputation, or of lost opportunities that might affect their future.

We need to be a bit realistic and recognise that establishing a corporate value or principle doesn't automatically mean that transparency will be the norm. As with the other behaviours and interactions in the Atomic Innovation model, we need to put some practices in place to facilitate greater transparency amongst our colleagues.

———

Implement a centralised system where regular updates on all potential, in-progress and completed work can be made visible to everyone in the organisation at all times. There are many digital platforms that can help with this and will be particularly important if you are an organisation distributed across more than one physical location. If you are a smaller company and all in one spot, try picking a wall and using physical index cards to get started. It doesn't have to be fancy, it just needs to give all your people access to regular work status updates when they are unable to attend your live events. If you have or are planning to implement a job-related experiment board like the one we discussed in the chapter on Creativity, then extend that same system to include all of your work.

Mandate that each team update this centralised system on a frequency that makes sense for the type of work they do and measure their adherence to this policy. The team may produce an incredibly creative and imaginative output, but if they haven't been open and transparent with the rest of the organisation along the way, they may have missed out on a piece of feedback or insight that could have made it even better. Not every piece of work will have enough useful information to update weekly, so you'll need to figure out what frequency works for you.

Don't worry too much if the number of people excited about consuming this type of information on a regular basis is low, especially at first. You will have a collection of people who just love to know what's going on and are looking for opportunities to get involved. Ask these early-adopters to be vocal about what they learn with their colleagues as a method of spreading the practice more broadly amongst your staff.

———

Make it a requirement of all leaders in the company that they actively walk the floors and talk to people about what they are doing on some regular frequency. Ask them to spend time with people and demonstrate genuine interest about initial drafts of documents they are working on, early versions of prototypes that are being developed, or thinking behind decisions they are in the process of making.

It may take time for some of your employees to get comfortable with this idea, so leaders will need to make sure that people don't feel as if they are being monitored or scrutinised in any way. Tell everyone in advance that you are starting this practice, and why. Make it clear that this in no way reduces the level of autonomy they have to achieve goals in whatever way they think is best. Explain that they are not being judged on the quality or completion of their work, but rather that this is a way for leaders in the organisation to better collaborate with them directly.

This type of activity promotes transparency in two ways. First, and most obvious, is it gets people comfortable with the practice of sharing information before it is perfect, and with letting others know what they are doing, and why. The more everyone gets used to this idea, the earlier they open themselves up to new insight and feedback that can benefit the outcomes they are trying to achieve. Second, this activity makes leaders more accessible to everyone. It gives them the opportunity to directly interact with those whom they may not have regular face-to-face contact, where they can directly expand their knowledge about what's going on around the organisation in order to share what they've learned with their own teams and people.

———

It's an unfortunate reality in some organisations that face-time with a senior leader is seen as necessary to career advancement. It's also unfortunate that some people tend to listen more attentively to messages if they are communicated from a position of hierarchical authority. It shouldn't be that way, but if it is within your company, use it to your advantage to improve transparency.

Implement a regular project podcast or lecture series where senior leaders have short, unscripted discussions with people and teams about the work they are doing. Using whatever media works best for you, make these conversations available to everyone in the organisation. Cover topics such as why the work is important, how it aligns with strategic goals, what has been learned, processes that are being employed, and issues that they are dealing with. Allow questions from an audience to stimulate conversation, and give raw, honest answers as much as possible.

Prior to each event in the series, have the senior leader who will be facilitating the conversation join the team in delivering the piece of work. I mean literally join the team, not figuratively. It helps maintain a degree of authenticity when the senior organisational leader is treated like any other member of the team. Have this work be outside the normal area of focus for that leader, which potentially introduces more opportunities for cross-organisational collaboration.

———

Of course, there will be times when sensitivity around a particular topic is necessary. Perhaps it's to protect a critical trade secret or competitive advantage, as a requirement of an agreement with a partner or supplier, or for some other reason where the risk of someone finding out is considered so great that the topic must remain need-to-know. Carefully consider, and try to limit, the number of times this call is made so that the maximum number of people in your business are as informed as they can be.

By including a focus on transparency as a way of improving collaboration, we get a collection of people who feel more connected to the organisation, the work they are doing, and each other. It's a fundamental component in getting us to the innovative culture we hope to attain.

9

TRUST QUARK

COLLABORATION NEUTRON

Trust: *The belief that someone will do what they say, to the best of their ability, without intentionally harming another.*

Let's get this out of the way first. I'm not suggesting the level of trust one might have with a parent, spouse, or some other cherished confidant in their personal life. Often this word can get thrown around in a work setting without a clear definition of what we actually mean and how it affects the interaction between colleagues.

The level of trust we should be trying to achieve with our colleagues doesn't need to be any more complicated than the definition above. Do we think the other person will put all their effort into doing the thing to which they committed? Are we comfortable that they won't purposefully impact us or anyone else in a negative way while they do it?

From the perspective of the person who is trying to earn trust, it's our job to make sure our colleagues can answer both of those questions with a "yes". We can do this by being good at understanding the outcomes to which we are committing before we start, and by being even better at saying no when that clarity is not forthcoming, or if we know it's not possible to deliver what is expected. You may lose a bit of short-term favour with a colleague by declining a piece of work you know you can't deliver, but you won't lose trust. In fact, you have the opportunity to turn such a situation into a positive experience by offering to help that colleague redefine their expectations so that the answer becomes "yes", thereby retaining both the trust and favour that can be useful in maintaining long-term working relationships.

The other side of that coin is the person that needs to do the trusting. When we first start working with someone new about which we have no background, or with which we have no history, there is no reason we should trust them. They haven't earned it yet. Someone in the organisation, however, considers them a trustworthy asset otherwise they wouldn't (or shouldn't) be employed there. So, what should we do to help others earn our trust at work? The RiseBeyond.org website calls out a key component when they say: "Collaboration requires trust, and trust comes from reliability and consistency."[28] I would add respect and credibility to the mix as well. What we should be willing to do, by default, is respect everyone we work with enough to provide them with opportunities to gain credibility by being reliable and consistent. As they do, our trust in them will grow.

On the surface, it may appear challenging to make the fragile concept of trust something objectively measurable, or to put in place practices that specifically cause its emergence. If you can start with a clear definition, however, you'll find it's not as difficult as you think to find ways to manufacture trust between colleagues in a tangible way.

———

When deciding whether to place your trust in a colleague, a critical factor will be the importance of the work, and what's at stake if something goes wrong[29]. We can use this fact to our advantage as we work to increase trust throughout the organisation.

Require that your people break work down into the smallest possible pieces they can get away with. If they need to make a decision, ask them to turn that into a series of smaller decisions where each one informs the next. If they are launching a new product or service, require them to release in small versions on which they can iterate and build over time. If they are experimenting with an idea to improve their role, mandate that those experiments don't affect the whole system until there is evidence that it's working.

As a leader, insist on these kinds of practices and constantly challenge your people to make things smaller. Instead of demanding large plans that make significant predictions of future outputs, ask to be shown why a thing is as small as it can get, and how future iterations might be impacted by what they learn through each step.

Of course, decisions still need to consider the broader context, product releases still need to be aligned to the longer-term vision, and job-related experiments need to take the whole system into account. But spending time making things as small as they can be will make it easier for people and teams to trust each other because any potentially negative consequences are correspondingly reduced.

Require that all decisions be made based on evidence and supporting data. Yes, there will always be a "first decision", but even that is typically informed by information that already exists (we'll discuss this more in the chapter on Operational Space). This changes the trust relationship because people no longer need to necessarily trust the person making a decision. What they need to trust are the techniques used to gather and interpret data and insights.

This doesn't mean that experience and expertise aren't held in high regard. They are critical to the process of quickly and accurately assessing the data and insights gathered and figuring out how to respond. What it does mean is that people can put their trust in objective evidence rather than subjective workplace relationships.

When someone has performed a task for you, ask them to describe the data and insight used to inform any decisions made. If you are using a centralised system to keep everyone informed like we discussed in the chapter on Transparency, require that decisions are publicised there along with the supporting evidence. This doesn't take away the autonomy people have in achieving an agreed outcome however they see fit. It only requires that they show the processes and techniques they used in figuring out how to achieve it.

Essentially, this type of approach uses the human as a proxy for what is actually being trusted (the data and insight) until the human trust is established. In other words, I may have just met you, and therefore have no reason to trust you. But, I can respect you enough to assume you will base your decisions on data and insight that I do trust.

———

When dealing with the issue of trust between work colleagues, what if we started by eliminating some instances where high levels of trust are necessary, just to hold us over until such time as those levels exist? Sometimes it's not about increasing the output, but rather reducing the expectation.

When faced with a situation where you need to work with someone whose trust you have not yet gained, or who has not yet earned yours, change the parameters by working together to complete what-ever needs to be done. Often, trust concerns arise because someone is going away to do something on your behalf and you just need to hope that they deliver on what is promised. By being right there with them, you take this uncertainty away and greatly reduce - if not eliminate - the need to trust them.

If you hold a position of influence in the resourcing of work, take any lack of an existing working relationship between people into account when allocating them to complete it. Where possible, set it up so that those people are forced to work together for the period of time that the task is in progress. If you adopt the previous suggestion about making things as small as possible, the impact on time and resourcing can be kept to a minimum.

What you get in return is an accelerated increase in the level of mutual trust between those people, making all future resourcing decisions easier.

———

Enabling and supporting this fundamental component of the Atomic Innovation model can be a bit tricky due to the emotional nature of one person trusting another. Therefore, any actions you put into place won't be as effective as they could be, or could possibly make things worse, if you don't get to the heart of what it means to trust in your company, and in your people. Spend time with your colleagues to understand their view and do whatever you can to make it more than a word that gets thrown around without a clear definition.

Trust is critical to the process of people working together on things that could be considered innovative, which makes it a significant contributing factor in reaching our goal of a widespread culture of innovation.

PART IV

10

ENTREPRENEURSHIP ELECTRON

Ever since Eric Ries, in his book The Lean Startup, popularised the idea that "entrepreneur" could refer to someone in an established organisation as much as it could a person working on a startup[30], the word has been thrown around a lot when talking about corporate innovation. There is a spirit associated with entrepreneurship that businesses want to capture and support in their people, and with good reason. Some well-known people who have done some pretty amazing things come to mind when you think of entrepreneurs, so why not want to try and emulate that outcome. If done without specifying what is actually meant by the word, however, we can cause confusion among the people of whom that spirit is expected. That confusion leads to debates about whether the concept of entrepreneurship belongs in the corporate world at all.

We definitely need to think beyond the simple view that to be an entrepreneur, you must leave an existing corporation and set up an independent business venture. Why can't we treat our people as if they are doing just that inside the organisation? In a 2012 Forbes article, entrepreneurs are described as those who identify any need and fill it[31]. Sometimes, the best way to fill a need is to start a new business, while other times it may simply be to incrementally improve an internal corporate process. Whatever the case, we can leverage the same entrepreneurial traits, such as comfort with uncertainty, identification of opportunities, and building networks[32] as we work to make any vision a reality.

Entrepreneurship: *Taking the initiative and risk to turn a unique vision of the future into something tangible.*

It would be difficult to deliver true innovation without the abilities embodied by entrepreneurs. Why? Because innovation means we are doing things that haven't been done before, which involves an inherent level of uncertainty and risk. Your biggest risk could be financial (if starting a new business), but it could simply be to your time (if trying to improve how your job is done). The things most uncertain could revolve around whether customers actually care if you solve a particular problem, but it could just as easily be whether the benefit of a small improvement is worth the effort to implement it. Entrepreneurship, in any environment, is embracing that uncertainty, finding ways to quickly validate assumptions to reduce it, and creating valuable propositions in spite of it.

To be specific, we are talking about delivery here. Not the limited "Someone wrote a business case, now go create a plan and run this project" view of delivery. Those can be facilitated by someone with good project management skills to keep things on track. I'm talking about the entire end-to-end process associated with taking a concept to market by remaining nimble and navigating the terrain encountered along the way. This requires an entrepreneurial mindset and capability, driven by a passion to achieve the desired outcome in any way possible. From the moment you decide to pursue an idea or build a business, you are in delivery mode. There are many natural phases you will go through while doing it, but don't think of what you are doing as anything other than delivery just because you may not be "building" anything yet. Keeping this in mind will help your organisation properly resource and support the work undertaken to maintain momentum and flow from one phase to another.

Now that we've defined what we mean by entrepreneurship, we need to think creatively about what policies, practices and measures we can put in place to bring out the spirit and mindset in everyone throughout our organisations.

———

Teach everyone in your organisation techniques for rapid experimentation, and how to embed them into their delivery approach as they move from early concept to robust solution. Make it a requirement that all work utilise these techniques as a way of gaining evidence to validate or invalidate assumptions, thereby reducing the uncertainty associated with whether or not a piece of work might deliver the intended value.

Set an expectation that these experiments will be run in-market whenever possible, with the details and results made available to everyone in the central system we talked about in the chapter on Transparency. By the way, "in-market" simply means "with actual customers", so it applies as much to an internal process improvement as it does to a new product offering.

If you are a leader in your organisation, stop asking people if their project is on track. Instead, ask things like "What is the next experiment you are going to run, and what do you hope to learn from it?" Follow up with "How will that help you decide if it's worth doing any more?" Those in positions of influence can have a significant impact on what people do, and how they work, simply by changing the information requested from them.

The goal is for our people to be more entrepreneurial; to take the initiative and risk to turn a unique vision into something real. That's more likely to happen if what they are accountable for is gaining evidence that things should continue or stop and using experimental methods to obtain it as quickly as possible.

————

Treat every piece of work in your company like a startup business, making the people working on it full-time "equity-holding partners", with one person as the "CEO". I don't mean figuratively thinking like a startup - I mean literally treat them as an independent business, with the broader organisation as an investor (and depending on the work, a delivery partner). If you haven't yet done it, stop forming steering committees and replace them with "board members", with a chair instead of a sponsor.

This significantly changes the day-to-day working relationship between the team and the rest of the organisation, transferring more authority and responsibility to the people doing the work. Sure, the board of any business is the real boss, but in this structure, it's the team who find and elect their own board members. How empowering would it be if your team identify and select the people they think would be best to help lead them, no matter what their role is in the company? It's certainly more empowering than having a steering committee created based on title and placement in an organisational chart that is forced upon the team.

From a finance perspective, your organisation is no longer funding a piece of work. Instead, you are investing in a "business" and in the future-state they are trying to achieve, just as if you were investing in an actual independent startup - and you are treated just the same.

If the work is to create a new product or service,

then it's possible these teams will be permanently together as they continue to iterate and improve what is created. At some point, they will come back looking for the next round of funding, and the organisation can decide if it's worth it based upon the performance of that creation. The concept of a project ending in a traditional sense no longer exists, so it will force you to make sure the right people are on the team from the very beginning and invest in those pieces of work differently than you may have in the past.

Even when you must have specific projects of limited term, this model provides the best level of autonomy to the team. When the work is done, they can pitch and figuratively "sell" what they've built back to the organisation, assuming what they are trying to sell is worth the purchase price.

———

Extending the previous suggestion, give everyone in your organisation an amount of virtual money to invest in ideas or projects they believe in, and reward them based on the performance of those pieces of work. Those people become "shareholders", which makes the team running the project accountable to them just as they would be to any other real shareholder who has invested actual cash.

If the project generates revenue, the "investors" are paid "returns" against their investment. If the piece of work is a cost savings measure, reward the figurative shareholders with a return corresponding to progress against the savings goal. Allow the accumulation of non-expiring virtual returns which people can re-invest in future work or spend in a company store - maybe as part of a partner discount program that most larger organisations already have in place.

People running projects can then constantly seek funding in the form of virtual investment by their colleagues. The more investment, the more support is committed by the organisation to help things grow. Perhaps the teams running the work can exchange this virtual investment for more real cash from the organisation, or for more people to join the team.

While this can be an exciting way to get everyone in the business involved in innovative activities, the actual targets of this exercise are the teams and "CEOs" running the work. It further supports the concept that they are setting up and running a new startup business by mimicking real-world scenarios to drive entrepreneurial behaviour.

————

Just as an atom of regular matter is most stable when it has a full outer shell of electrons[33], Innovation Atoms are most stable when supported by solid entrepreneurial capability. Organisations can grow that capability by rethinking and redesigning the way work is funded, resourced and run to more closely mirror the world where entrepreneurs tend to thrive.

Innovation is not a guaranteed output of entrepreneurship, but we need to leverage the entrepreneurial spirit if we are to ever achieve the innovative culture that this model is set up to help create.

PART V

11

THE FORCES

There wouldn't be any stable atoms of regular matter in our universe if not for two of the forces that operate within them. It's the strong force, carried by Gluons, that binds quarks together inside protons and neutrons, and those together to form atomic nuclei. We also have the electromagnetic force to thank for keeping electrons in shells around that nucleus. It would be a bad day from the perspective of things made of matter if either one of those forces disappeared tomorrow.

To continue the atomic analogy, Innovation Atoms require that a couple of forces exist for us to make use of the behaviours, interactions and capabilities described by the model. Without them, we won't be able to bring those components together in a way that makes innovation an inevitable output of our everyday work.

So, what are the key forces in the Atomic Innovation model?

Courage Force: Binds the behaviour and interaction quarks together inside the Vision Proton and the Collaboration Neutron, while keeping those together to form an Innovation Atom nucleus.

Excitement Force: Keeps the Entrepreneurship Electron in orbit around an Innovation Atom nucleus.

Without these forces to hold things in place, the fundamental particles that make up an Innovation Atom would just float around, randomly bumping into each other, and only occasionally in a combination that causes innovation as a measurable output.

We can cause an innovative culture to emerge by supporting the use of these forces as much as we can, while guarding against other corporate forces that might conspire to tear things apart.

12

COURAGE FORCE

THE FORCES

Courage: *The strength to act in the face of fear or uncertainty.*

"It was really brave the way you spoke up in that meeting." "Trying an idea like that took a lot of courage." Hopefully, you've heard phrases like these spoken amongst your colleagues. Perhaps you've even said them yourself or had them said to you.

In everyday language, we often think of courage and bravery as being two words describing the same thing. From a philosophical perspective, however, they are not. Bravery is a persistent quality that exists in the absence of fear, while courage is taking action to reach an outcome despite the presence of fear[34]. It's for this reason that courage, as described in the philosophical sense, is used as the force that brings behaviours and interactions together in the Atomic Innovation model.

Most people would agree that it takes courage to start new things. This is especially true the earlier you are in delivering a piece of innovative work, as that's typically when the most uncertainty, and potentially the most fear, exists. We can't forget, however, that it takes as much courage to persist as it does to kick off in the first place. The Psychology Today website, in a list of quotes on courage, includes a good one from Mary Anne Radmacher: "Courage doesn't always roar. Sometimes courage is the little voice at the end of the day that says I'll try again tomorrow."[35]

For as much courage as it takes to get started and keep going, it takes as much or more to act upon moments where there is a need to stop doing something. Perhaps you've decided it's time to kill a project before it's finished, or significantly change direction. It's hard to tell someone else that an idea they've supported is no longer a good one to pursue, and even harder when the person you need to convince is yourself. As you experiment more and more with potentially innovative ideas, however, the number of moments like that will increase.

This is the most difficult part of the Atomic Innovation model, and unfortunately, you don't get many shots at getting it right. Feeling that there could be a negative impact on their reputation in response to a courageous act will cause a person to hesitate before doing so again. That's a bad outcome for the person as well as the organisation, so we need to take this seriously and dedicate time to finding the best ways of bringing out and supporting the right kind of courage in our people.

———

Make it ok to get things wrong, or for things to not work as expected. Some will refer to this as "celebrating failure", but let's be honest; nobody enjoys feeling like they've failed at something. If you insist on using that word, then be very clear what you mean by it in different circumstances. For example, invalidating a hypothesis would be a great "failure" to celebrate, but purposefully ignoring risky assumptions and delivering anyway - not so much.

Document these learnings where everyone can see them, talk honestly about what happened and why, and do it right after it happens. This keeps the conversations fresh and gives everyone else the opportunity to benefit from this new knowledge by potentially making use of it in their own work. Make it a badge of honour; kind of like the Purple Heart[36] of the business world. Perhaps even hand out awards for spectacular "failures" that have resulted in the organisation being that much more knowledgeable about its people, its industry, and its customers.

Most importantly, once you've documented and discussed it, let it go. No matter how well they are celebrated, people don't like to be reminded of things in the past that didn't work. If people think they are going to be constantly reminded of things that didn't go well in the past or feel as if they might be excluded from an opportunity in the future because of it, you run the risk of killing the courage you are trying to support before it has a chance to happen.

———

There are few fears with more influence over a willingness to display courage than the impact on personal income. Excluding the very small number of independently wealthy who work just for the fun of it, the rest of us work because we need a source of income and can be quite shy about risking it.

Separate all compensation conversations from delivery of specific, pre-determined outputs. Instead, if you must compensate people based on work delivered, then align it to the outcome desired. People in your organisation will be more willing to experiment in the quest for innovative outputs if their financial position isn't impacted by what happens. Even if this isn't the most important factor to some individual people, you've taken away one critical thing that could have been holding others back.

If your organisation is willing to take the leap, completely remove the concept of associating compensation with work done. There are better, more progressive ways of measuring a person's contribution to the business than simply "did that project get delivered on scope, time and budget?" If you pay bonuses or incentives, figure out what you typically distribute to each person, add it to their salary, and be done with it. You will now have the best paid people, giving you the ability to hire the best quality people, who can courageously help you achieve an innovative business culture.

———

It's not just fear of failure that requires a bit of courage to face. It also takes courage to display the behaviours and leverage the interactions described by the Atomic Innovation model in the first place. Sometimes, people need a little nudge to show them that it's safe.

Regularly have one team run their piece of work in a public space. Perhaps you are in a large building with an open foyer, or if that's not an option, use a kitchen or other shared space in your office. Have them use it the same as they would any other working space in the building by relocating there, holding meetings and showcases visible to everyone, and displaying hypotheses and experiment results on the walls.

What these teams will start to realise is that their colleagues are there to help and support them, and that it's safe to put their work, and themselves, on display for all their colleagues to see. The more people get exposure to this fact, the more courageous they are likely to be in future work because they've been through it already.

You'll need to tell everyone why you are doing this, so they will know that it's ok to interact with the teams on display. Also, set an expectation that leaders in your organisation will regularly visit these teams and talk about the progress of their work. The effects of this approach won't be as strong if the team is visible but not engaged by their colleagues.

———

There is a difference between courage and ego, and we should set a goal to not inadvertently reward the latter. Courage can be associated with being bold, but a question must be asked: is the judgement of boldness due to a humble action in the face of uncertainty, or because of a craving for attention. There is a very real danger that organisations can inadvertently cause the latter to occur through their methods of recognition and reward. As you work out the best ways to support courage in your people, take care to ensure that only those people displaying real versions of it are celebrated, and not simply those seeking the most attention.

It takes courage to trust people. It takes courage to be transparent. It's required to put your creativity and imagination on display for all to see. It's an important thing that can sometimes require examples from others before being exhibited by one's self.

Without it, however, the behaviours and interactions of this model are just characteristics floating free without the structure necessary to bring about constant and consistent levels of innovation.

13

EXCITEMENT FORCE

THE FORCES

Excitement: *A feeling of enthusiasm or eagerness.*

In an earlier chapter, we discussed the important role that an entrepreneurial mindset and capability plays in the Atomic Innovation model. But what attracts people like that to a piece of work, and keeps them there during the ups and downs that are bound to be encountered?

It's the excitement associated with doing something new and different. It's the feeling of enthusiasm for tackling important customer and business problems, and an eagerness to deliver innovative solutions that solve them. Entrepreneurs, whether building a startup or working within a corporate, get excited by the challenge of doing something that hasn't been done before. By providing our people with opportunities to take on those challenges within our organisations, we generate the excitement needed to keep people focused on creating innovative outputs, leading to the culture we are trying to achieve.

A 2016 Forbes article states that the excitement of an entrepreneurial life isn't derived from specific activities, but rather from a way of thinking, believing, and viewing the world[37]. While the context of that article was starting a new business, the same is true for entrepreneurs within established organisations. It's not the micro that matters; the detailed list of tasks to be done. Instead, it's the macro view; the "what could be", that people get excited about. Once excited about delivering a piece of work, people will have no problem finding things to do because of the accompanying drive to make it real.

Some people get excited by belief in a strong corporate purpose, or by clear company positions on important social matters where they want to make a difference. Others are driven by the potential for rewards and public recognition. Each company is comprised of a unique set of complementary personalities, with their own points-of-view on what makes work exciting, and their own reasons for loving what they do. It's important that an organisation understand what makes their people tick in order to find creative ways of increasing the level of excitement they feel while doing their work.

Despite this uniqueness, however, there are some basic things you can do to start generating a level of excitement for innovation throughout your organisation.

————

Actively publicise your innovation efforts to the entire organisation, and to the rest of the world. Create a regular schedule of recurring press releases outlining all of the innovative concepts that are being explored, or have recently been delivered, by your organisation.

Depending on the type of work being pursued, you may need different versions for internal versus external audiences. For internal ones, include everything that you can. It's possible that there is specific work going on that needs to be kept confidential, even amongst your staff, but keep that distinction as a rarely used special case.

Make it the responsibility of one group within your company to own this process and measure them on the frequency and quality of publication. If you can, choose people from different teams, and develop the message from their perspective (just be sure they are the type of person who enjoys the attention).

If you're spending all this time on organisation-wide innovation efforts, why not spread the word? Most of your people will be grateful for the airtime, and it might just help with your recruitment efforts as well. If nothing else, it will hopefully put some fear into your competitors.

———

Run regular innovation challenges for your employees and partners. Pick a customer or business problem space that will resonate with your people, and invite them to collaborate in small, self-forming teams to find innovative solutions and develop experiments to test them. Make it clear that it doesn't matter what role they currently occupy, or the area of the business in which they currently work. The goal is to provide opportunities for everyone to learn new skills, work with different people, and develop their capabilities in a way that might not be possible in their regular job.

Make sure you have coaching and other support readily available to help teams learn and use your preferred approach to concept experimentation and development. If necessary, bring in outside help to run these events. The most important thing is to ensure the experience for participants is a good one. If it isn't, the likelihood that they will participate in future challenges is low.

The duration of time over which these types of challenges will run can vary, so you'll have to try a few different options to find the ones that work. This could range from a couple of days to several months, depending on the size of the problem space, and the fidelity of the outputs you want to have at the end. No matter what you decide, always finish it off with a session where participating teams can pitch their concepts to the entire organisation. This gives teams a chance to showcase not only their work, but also their capability, which raises their profile amongst their colleagues.

You'll need full, public support for this type of thing from the highest levels within your organisation. Without it, your people won't know that they are permitted to prioritise involvement over other things they could be doing, and you run the risk of not actually delivering any good concepts that emerge from it.

———

Develop a program to reward people unexpectedly, and in different ways. This should go beyond ordinary financial incentives and be set up in such a way that the criteria for reward is equally achievable by everyone in each area of the company. The last thing you want to do is have a reward that only certain roles in the same area of the business can achieve simply due to the nature of their work.

If you are not sure where to start, survey your staff and ask them about the last time they were excited at work, and what was going on at the time to cause it. Create a backlog of your findings, prioritise them, and treat the process of developing this rewards program exactly the same as you would any other idea or concept. Run quick experiments to test the impact of different possible rewards and iterate them over time.

As we've discussed previously in this book, innovation goes beyond products and services, so that means we can use the same techniques to identify and roll out innovative rewards to generate excitement in people for their work, and for the organisation as a whole.

———

It's a great feeling when you enjoy your work. Quality tends to be higher when people come to the office energised by what they are doing, and excited about what will be achieved if it works. Overall job satisfaction increases as a result, which for some, can have a direct impact on their physical and mental well-being[38]. Plus, if people are excited about what they are doing, they are likely to share that excitement with others, making it easier for your organisation to recruit the type of people for whom the behaviours and interactions described in this book come naturally.

It's the last piece in the structure of an Innovation Atom, and critical to sustaining a constant level of innovation. Without it, we have nothing to keep our Entrepreneurship Electron in place, and nothing to keep our people who embody the entrepreneurial spirit from searching for that excitement within some other organisation.

PART VI

PART VI

14

OPERATIONAL SPACE

As you would have noticed, most of the techniques that I've suggested in this book for enabling the behaviours and interactions represented by the Atomic Innovation model have to do with changing how you work. To get to a point where innovation is an inevitable output of our daily work, we need to be open to potentially changing every part of our organisation's operating model.

You might ask: "How can I innovate my ways of working, if my ways of working don't support innovation?" Does this create what can be referred to as a "chicken and egg" scenario? Yes, it does, but not in the way people usually mean when uttering that phrase. Typically, people say that as a way of describing a situation where there are two things dependent on each other for their very existence, and therefore it's unclear how one precedes the other. Fortunately, we can again look to Neil DeGrasse Tyson for clarification, who gave us this post on Twitter:

"Just to settle it once and for all: Which came first the Chicken or the Egg? The Egg -- laid by a bird that was not a Chicken"[39]

Innovation is our egg, and the organisation's current operating model is our chicken. Just as there is no single moment in time where you go from Bird-That-Is-Not-A-Chicken to Chicken, you don't end the work day with an operating model that doesn't support innovative outputs and show up the next morning with a new one that does. Both of these things evolve slowly over time, and you don't notice it while it's happening. Only much later can you look back and arbitrarily call out a distinction.

Focus on what you can do today to enable the behaviours, interactions and capabilities that bring innovative outputs to life. Do whatever you can within your current ways of working to create as many Innovation Atoms as you can. Lay enough of these eggs, and eventually, one hatches that you'll be able to reflect on one day and call a chicken.

If you are in a leadership position within your organisation or have some influence over how people work, question operational practices that could restrict flexibility or limit the ability to make new things happen quickly. Run some experiments of your own on your operating model to see if you can move the dial in a positive direction on a few of them.

For example:

How are decisions made in your company? What would you need to do to enable everyone in the organisation to make and implement decisions on their own? What information would you need to provide to people in order for this to happen? Would your organisational or operational structures need to change as a result?

How do you choose what to work on? What would it take to make that process more dynamic and fluid? Could you create a sustainable, continuous process of constantly identifying and prioritising new problems to solve? What parts of how you allocate resources and funding to work would need to change in order to pull this off?

How is success and failure measured? Could you create an environment where people feel comfortable trying things that might not work? Would your leadership style need to be different to enable this kind of mindset? How would the management of projects need to change to support ongoing learning through rapid experiments? What methods of communication would you need to employ to share those learnings more broadly?

The answers to these types of questions must be determined within the context of your organisation. If you're not sure how to begin, the process of answering them can be accelerated by bringing in some outside help from people who have done this kind of thing before. Make sure, however, that those you bring in to help are coming up with the answers, and designing any necessary changes, with you - not for you. For any changes to be effective and lasting, any external party must be embedded alongside your people for some period of time so that they can design them together. If the outside help really has done this before, they'll know that an iterative, experimental approach is just as powerful for this type of work as it is when launching a new product to market.

———

Take care that, while thinking you are creating better ways of working, you inadvertently end up making everyone's work more difficult to complete. Most of the time when this happens, it's because the organisation holds on for dear life to an older thought process while simultaneously attempting to implement something new. As an example, this model promotes collaboration as critical to innovation, but that doesn't mean complete consensus. I've seen many instances where, in an attempt to seem collaborative, people run around getting the opinion of too many people so that everyone is "across" whatever they are doing. All this does is slow things down, demotivate teams and make them feel less empowered. Another example is when first adopting design-led and experimental methods of ideation and delivery, organisations can try to force antiquated techniques of project, portfolio and financial management on top of them. The benefit of these modern ways of working is that they eliminate the need for much of this overhead because the reduction of risk is an innate part of their design.

Some of the recommendations in this book reference freeing up a portion of people's working time to participate in activities that may not be part of their role today. Whether it's being invited to participate in the ideation process being conducted by others or taking time to experiment with ways to improve how people do their own job, freeing up this capacity is crucial to influencing whether we ultimately achieve an innovative culture, or not. Use caution that this doesn't become an "in addition to your full-time job" scenario, because no one will do it. You need it to be an "as part of your full-time job" kind of thing. If people only have time by giving up their lunch breaks or working extra hours, then you've failed in your execution. Constant and consistent messaging from leaders that people have the freedom to use some of their normal work time in this way will be a critical part of making innovation a reality.

The ongoing work associated with innovating your operational space will not be free from challenges. It's possible that not everyone you work with will think this a good thing to do. Some areas of the business will seem much too complicated to change. Partners may not be able to keep up. Be bold but patient, and don't give up. For an innovative culture to emerge, we must be open to potentially changing anything and everything about how we work.

What do we get in return for all this effort? An organisation where people want to work because of how we do it, that makes money because of how we spend it, and that competitors fear because of our action in the face of it.

15

CULTURAL UNIVERSE

While making your way through this book, it's possible you thought to yourself: "Our people already exhibit these behaviours. We trust each other and are completely transparent, but we're not seeing the level of innovation you are talking about." There are two reasons why that could be true. First, it's possible you're being more innovative than you thought, and just haven't realised it yet. Second, and more likely, is that the ways of working adopted by your organisation are restricting the level of innovation you are trying to achieve.

My experience is that innovation efforts fail when businesses don't fully realise, or aren't fully committed to, all that it takes to achieve it. This doesn't necessarily mean that you are investing large chunks of money in it at the beginning, or ever. It can be unfair to compare your own commitment to the biggest companies in the world who tend to get the most press on this topic. Some of those companies have so much money that they can throw large sums over the innovation fence and have enough remaining that it doesn't really seem to matter. That is not true for the majority of companies out there. Your organisation will need to figure out how much money and time it's willing to spend to deliver innovative outputs, and to what extent you want an innovative mindset to permeate the organisation.

Just to be absolutely clear, there will certainly continue to be work you do that isn't considered innovative. Sometimes, the most appropriate thing to do will be to copy what's been done before, or make an obvious change, and move on. By applying this model, however, and by supporting the behaviours and interactions it describes, you are more likely to have innovative outputs as options, and more regularly. A decision to ignore them is then an informed choice that you make based on the scenario in which you find yourself at that time. This way, you have some control over, and can make some accurate predictions about, the level of innovation happening throughout your organisation.

The long-term goal is to claim ourselves as having a

culture of innovation. In order for that to happen, innovation needs to be a constant output of the work that we undertake on a daily basis. We won't produce that innovation unless we have a clear vision of how things could be better in the future, created by our collective curiosity, creativity, and imagination. We also won't get there if we are not collaborating effectively by communicating, being transparent, and trusting our colleagues. Once those components are established, we need an entrepreneurial mindset and capability to bring these visions to life and turn them into something tangible.

It's going to take some personal and professional courage to pull it off, but it's worth it because of the excitement associated with solving problems in ways they haven't been solved before, by using solutions in ways they've never been used before, to create experiences that are better than they've ever been before.

That's Atomic Innovation.

ATOMIC INNOVATION CANVAS

Not many people enjoy the process of writing business cases. They take tons of effort to create and are often filled with information and projections that everyone knows are complete guesses. No one ever really reads them in any detail, and when they do it's at the beginning of a piece of work when you don't know anything, or at the end when it's too late to do anything about it. One of the most liberating things leaders can do for their people is to eliminate the traditional practice of business casing.

There are modern documents we can use that are much more suited to design-led, iterative and experimental approaches to work that capture what we know, and highlight what we don't know, about a particular concept or idea. They help us to facilitate a prioritisation discussion about what work to experiment on next, and to give the team doing the work a clear description of what we are trying to achieve, and why. These documents are often called canvases, with the most common and well-known of these being the Lean Canvas[40], Business Model Canvas[41] and Value Proposition Canvas[42].

To support the model described in this book, I offer a new option: the Atomic Innovation Canvas. It's a single-page document derived from the structures of both the Business Model and Lean canvases designed to capture all the relevant information necessary to decide if we should pursue a piece of work, and how we will keep ourselves aligned to the goals associated with it. It doesn't matter if what you are planning to do is launch a new global product offering or make a small improvement to the way one person does their job. It's a place to document updated goals as we acquire new learnings, to help identify the big assumptions we are making so we can prioritise what to do next, and to communicate with the stakeholders what the world will look like when we are done. Most importantly, it doesn't need to be complete before exploration work on an idea begins. It's a document that gets filled out during the ideation process to determine if the concept is ulti-mately worth the effort it will take to deliver it.

The type of information captured in an Atomic Innovation Canvas is:

Vision: A short description of the future you are trying to create. Keep it simple and clear so that everyone doing the work can judge if their activities are aligned to making the vision a reality.

Problems We Will Solve: A list of the most important problems that you are going to solve for your customers. Be clear and specific about the problems you are solving, and make sure the problems you put in this box are ones experienced by the customers you list in the "Who We Are Solving Them For" box.

Who We Are Solving Them For: A list of the customer groups for whom you are solving the problems identified in the "Problems We Will Solve" box. Keep in mind that sometimes the customer is internal to your organisation. Try not to confuse who you are solving the problem "for" (those go here), and who you are solving the problem "with" (those go in the "Partners We Will Work With" box). Identify the customer group you are most likely to target first.

How They Are Solved Today: A list of the ways that the customer groups you've named currently deal with the problems that you've listed. Consider direct and indirect competitors in the market, as well as methods of dealing with the problems that customers may have come up with on their own.

How We Will Solve Them: A description, at a high level, of how you intend to solve the problems for the customer groups you've identified. Cover all the important aspects of your solution without getting into detail about specific features (unless they are a critical component of what you intend to do). Make sure the description of your solution covers all the problems you have listed.

How It's Better Than Alternatives: A description of the key and important ways that what you will deliver is better than what's listed in the "How They Are Solved Today" box. Focus on the differentiators that will cause customers to use your solution instead of what they do today.

Special Expertise We Need: A list of any specialist skills or expertise that will be needed to deliver and operate the solution you've described. Only worry about skills or expertise that you don't necessarily have ready access to (i.e. people you may need to train or hire).

Partners We Will Work With: A list of any other

people, teams or organisations you will work with to operate the solution you've described. Only worry about those who will help you operate your solution once it's delivered (not those who join you temporarily to help deliver it - those can go in the Specialist Expertise box).

How People Will Know About It: A list of the methods you intend to use to let your customers know that the new solution exists. Make sure the channels you put here are ones actually used by the customer groups listed.

Things That Will Cost Us Money (and How Much): A list of the things (people, systems, etc) that will cost you money to deliver and operate the solution you've described. Only worry about money you aren't already spending, such as costs associated with acquiring any of the specialist skills you listed. If you know how much something will cost, put that in as well (early in the ideation process, you may not know specific numbers).

How The Business Will Benefit (and How Much): If your solution generates revenue for the business, then it's a list of the ways in which you intend to generate that revenue. If your solution reduces expenses, then it's a description of how it will save the business money. It's also possible that the benefit to the business is not financial, such as a larger user base or improved perception in the market, so include that where appropriate. If you know the amounts associated with the benefit, then include those as well (early in the ideation process, you may not know specific numbers).

Why We Should Do It Now: A description of what (if any) customer or business benefit that would be lost if the idea is not pursued right away. Consider access to resources, trends in the market and competitor activity when deciding if there any risks associated with not doing this now. Be honest in your assessment of potential benefit loss, as this can help inform where the concept sits in the overall organisational priorities.

How We Will Know It's Working: A description of how you will quantifiably measure that your solution is actually solving the listed customer problems and delivering the expected business benefit. Make sure the results from your measurement methods can be directly attributable to your solution (Hint: you may need to deliver the ability to measure success as part of your solution if it doesn't already exist, so make sure to factor that in).

———

So, how do you use an Atomic Innovation Canvas most effectively within your organisation? Perhaps you are working with others on a program to explore a problem space, engaging customers directly to identify new ones that might be worth solving. Or, maybe you were at work today and decided that you just can't deal with some internal process or system anymore and want to do something about it.

Either way, the starting point is the same. The moment you have identified a problem to solve or have a new idea, start with a blank canvas and complete the sections as best you can. If the information you enter represents an assumption you are making, highlight that clearly in the document itself. If you're not sure where to start, focus first on the problems you are solving, and the customers for whom you are solving them. Then, complete as many of the other sections as you can. Even this basic attempt can be enough for you to decide if the idea is worth putting in any more effort to expanding upon it. Whatever you do, keep it simple, with plain language and just a few bullet points in each box. If you try and put a lot of text in each, it will only add unnecessary complexity to the document and make it more difficult to read.

Your ideation process can then be focused on completing all the remaining sections, replacing any risky assumptions with information based on data and evidence. That process, by the way, doesn't necessarily represent any particular amount of required effort or investment. For those new, fuzzy ideas where you don't know much at the beginning, it can take some time to gather all the information necessary to fill in all the sections. However, there will also be ideas where you already know a lot and can confidently complete the canvas in just a few minutes.

At some point, it will be necessary to prioritise the canvases you've created against each other so that you can focus your efforts on the right things at the right time. If you're new to this and not sure where to start, do this prioritisation after you've identified the problem you want to solve and what you believe to be the right solution to solve it, but before you've started serious experimentation in market. By doing so, you prevent people from spending too much time and money pursuing ideas that don't align to your strategy, while simultaneously promoting good concept development flow by putting the right teams in place early and then getting out of their way.

Essentially, the Atomic Innovation Canvas does three things for you:

1) It captures the information needed to make an informed decision about whether the piece of work should be pursued, and where it fits in the overall organisational priorities.

2) It gives the people doing the work a clear objective to which they can align all of their activities.

3) It provides a place to document updated information based on new learnings and knowledge obtained throughout the delivery process.

Templates for the Atomic Innovation Canvas, as well as samples of what a quality canvas looks like, are available for free at www.TenPercentLabs.com.

Title: My Coffee Joint		Author: Scott W.	Version: v2 5/4/18

Vision

Create the best coffee buying experience for environmentally-conscious people in a hurry.

Problems We Will Solve	Who We Are Solving Them For	How They Are Solved Today
A lot of money is spent every day for takeaway coffee.	People who pick up a coffee on their way in to work.	Make a coffee at home and bring it with them to work.
There is growing concern for the amount of non-recyclable waste generated by takeaway coffee cups.	People who leave work mid-morning or mid-afternoon for a coffee break.	Make a coffee when they get to work.
A significant amount of time is spent waiting for a coffee once it's been ordered.	First target: Business people who work in the city and pick up a coffee on their way to the office.	Carry around personal re-usable coffee mugs.
		Use digital tools to pre-order coffee in advance so it's waiting for them.

How We Will Solve Them

Open a cafe that pre-makes the most popular kind of coffees and keeps in a customer-accessible warmer to eliminate waiting.

Use 100% recyclable cups, lids and other accessories.

Sell advertising and sponsorships on all cups, lids, stirrers, etc.

Sell the coffee to customers at ingredient + labour cost.

How It's Better Than Alternatives

One less thing to do in the morning.

Don't have to clean and carry around a re-usable mug.

No wait time as coffee choices will be pre-made and waiting.

Significantly reduced cost to consumers.

Reduced landfill.

Special Expertise We Need	Partners We Will Work With	How People Will Know About It
Baristas.	Company to arrange advertising and sponsorship deals.	Foot traffic.
		Work of mouth.
		Advertising on public transport.
		Advertising parking facilities.

The Things That Will Cost Us Money (and How Much)	How The Business Will Benefit (and How Much)
Employees and management to operate shop locations: $30k - $40k / yr each	Sales of takeaway coffees (to cover cost): $2 per coffee
Facility costs (lease, insurance, pest management, etc): $48k / yr lease + other	Advertising / Sponsorship arrangements: $ TBD
Inventory: $ TBD	
Awareness (of shop, and with advertising/sponsorship partner): $ TBD	

Why We Should Do It Now	How We Will Know It's Working
Novelty of first to market.	Wait time for coffee pickup.
Increasing non-recyclable waste being produced.	Revenue from advertising and sponsorship deals.

THE ATOMIC INNOVATION HANDBOOK — ATOMIC INNOVATION CANVAS

MODEL BRAINSTORMING POSTER

Throughout each section of this book, I've included some suggestions on ways you might promote, support or otherwise enable the behaviours and interactions that are key to making the Atomic Innovation model work. As we've discussed, however, no one organisation can simply adopt the practices and policies of another without first considering the context in which they operate and figure out for themselves the best way to bring the model to life.

To help facilitate this process, I've included a template you can use to organise your own thoughts and ideas. Put this poster up on a wall, grab some sticky notes, and hold regular sessions with diverse groups of people to brainstorm ways to drive these behaviours and interactions in the day-to-day work throughout your organisation. Vote on and priori-tise the ones you think have the best chance of working and give people time to experiment with them in their roles, and with their colleagues.

Not all of your ideas will be successful, but that doesn't matter. Your effort will have been worth it when the innovative culture you've been after is finally a reality.

A template for the Behaviour and Interaction Ideas brainstorming poster is available for free at www.TenPercentLabs.com.

Vision		
Curiosity	**Creativity**	**Imagination**
A strong desire to learn and understand.	*Actively looking for ways to do things differently.*	*Seeking out that which is not currently obvious to the senses.*

Collaboration		
Communication	**Transparency**	**Trust**
The two way exchange of information and meaning.	*Full disclosure without hidden agendas or conditions.*	*The belief that one will do what they say, to the best of their ability, without intentionally harming another.*

Entrepreneurship	Forces	
	Excitement	**Courage**
Taking the initiative and risk to turn a unique vision of the future in to something tangible.	*A feeling of enthusiasm or eagerness.*	*The strength to act in the face of fear or uncertainty.*

THE ATOMIC INNOVATION HANDBOOK   **BEHAVIOUR AND INTERACTION IDEAS**

REFERENCES

1. Owen Gough (2017). How is loyalty changing the way we shop and compare brands. Accessed March 2018 through http://smallbusiness.co.uk/loyalty-changing-experience-brands-2540331/

2. Larry Alton (2018). Why the gig economy is the best and worst development for workers under 30. Accessed March 2018 through https://www.forbes.com/sites/larryalton/2018/01/24/why-the-gig-economy-is-the-best-and-worst-development-for-workers-under-30/#1c4440966d76

3. Volker Staack, Branton Cole (2017). Reinventing innovation, five findings to guide strategy through execution. Accessed March 2018 through

https://www.pwc.com/us/en/advisory-services/business-innovation/assets/2017-innovation-benchmark-findings.pdf

4. Tim Sharp (2017). What is an atom? Accessed March 2018 through https://www.livescience.com/37206-atom-definition.html

5. Duncan Bucknell (2013). The difference between a strategy, a plan, and a process. Accessed March 2018 through https://duncanbucknell.com/2013/04/12/the-difference-between-a-strategy-a-plan-and-a-process/

6. Ries, Eric. 2011. The Lean Startup: How today's entrepreneurs use continuous innovation to create radically successful businesses. (First Edition). United States: Crown Business

7. Adeo Ressi (2016). Create a clear vision for your business, and then stick to it. Accessed March 2018 through https://www.forbes.com/sites/adeoressi/2016/08/09/create-a-clear-vision-for-your-business-and-then-stick-to-it/#132c7a731d33

8. Barbara Farfan (2018). Amazon.com's mission statement. Accessed May 2018

through
https://www.thebalancesmb.com/amazon-mission-statement-4068548

9. No Name Found (2017). Best examples of company vision and mission statements. Accessed May 2018 through https://www.themarketingblender.com/vision-mission-statements/

10. Jay Yarow (2013) Here's Amazon's vision for the Kindle in 45 words. Accessed May 2018 through https://www.businessinsider.com.au/heres-amazons-vision-for-the-kindle-in-45-words-2013-1?r=US&IR=T

11. Celeste Kidd, Benjamin Y. Hayden (2015). The psychology and neuroscience of curiosity. Accessed March 2018 through http://www.cell.com/neuron/fulltext/S0896-6273(15)00767-9

12. No Name Found: N. (2015). The neuroscience behind curiosity and motivation. Accessed March 2018 through https://www.thecubelondon.com/portfolio/the-neuroscience-behind-curiosity-and-motivation/

13. No Name Found: N. (2017). 5 traits of successful tech startup founders. Accessed March 2018 through

https://www.rocketspace.com/tech-startups/5-traits-of-successful-tech-startup-founders

14. Bruce Kasanoff (2014). Why people (incorrectly) think they are not creative. Accessed March 2018 through https://www.forbes.com/sites/brucekasanoff/2014/05/15/why-people-think-they-are-not-creative/#22dfb77f26a3

15. Jennifer Mueller (2017). Chinese and American consumers have different ideas about what makes a product creative. Accessed March 2018 through https://hbr.org/2017/02/chinese-and-american-consumers-have-different-ideas-about-what-makes-a-product-creative

16. No Name Found: N. (2014). Stephen Colbert interviews Neil DeGrasse Tyson. Accessed March 2018 through https://www.youtube.com/watch?v=0Banc_-AyUc

17. Patrick Vlaskovits (2011). Henry Ford, innovation, and that "faster horse" quote. Accessed March 2018 through https://hbr.org/2011/08/henry-ford-never-said-the-fast

18. Clayton M. Christensen, Taddy Hall, Karen

Dillon, David S. Duncan (2016). Know your customer's "jobs to be done". Accessed March 2018 through https://hbr.org/2016/09/know-your-customers-jobs-to-be-done

19. No Name Found: N. No Date Found: s.d. 5 Whys. Accessed March 2018 through https://en.wikipedia.org/wiki/5_Whys

20. Ron Ashkenas (2015). There's a difference between cooperation and collaboration. Accessed March 2018 through https://hbr.org/2015/04/theres-a-difference-between-cooperation-and-collaboration

21. Robert J. Thomas (2011). The three essential ingredients of great collaborations. Accessed March 2018 through https://hbr.org/2011/06/the-three-essential-ingredient

22. No Name Found: N. No Date Found: s.d. 14 management principles of the Toyota Way. Accessed March 2018 through http://leanblitzconsulting.com/14-principles-of-the-toyota-way/

23. Cynthia K. West. No Date Found: s.d. Four common reasons why projects fail. Accessed March 2018 through

https://www.projectinsight.net/white-papers/four-common-reasons-why-projects-fail

24. Jane [Surname Unknown] (2017). 9 effective communication skills. Accessed March 2018 through https://www.habitsforwellbeing.com/9-effective-communication-skills/

25. Alison Doyle (2018). Communication skills for workplace success. Accessed March 2018 through https://www.thebalance.com/communication-skills-list-2063779

26. No Name Found: N. (2017). Why transparency is vital to engaging millennial employees. Accessed April 2018 through https://unito.io/blog/transparency-is-vital-to-engaging-millennials/

27. No Name Found: N. No Date Found: s.d. Company Values. Accessed March 2018 through https://www.atlassian.com/company/values

28. No Name Found: N. No Date Found: s.d. 6 skills needed for effective collaboration. Accessed April 2018 through https://www.risebeyond.org/6-skills-needed-for-effective-collaboration/

29. Nan S Russell (2013). How to decide if your should trust someone at work. Accessed April 2018 through https://www.psychologytoday.com/us/blog/ trust-the-new-workplace- currency/201308/how-decide-if-you- should-trust-someone-work

30. Ries, Eric. 2011. The Lean Startup: How today's entrepreneurs use continuous innovation to create radically successful businesses. (First Edition). United States: Crown Business, pp. 26-27

31. Brett Nelson (2012). The real definition of entrepreneur—and why it matters. Accessed April 2018 through https://www.forbes.com/sites/brettnelson/2 012/06/05/the-real-definition-of- entrepreneur-and-why-it- matters/#23144f4e4456

32. Marissa Levin (2017). The 5 skills and behaviours that make entrepreneurs successful, according to Harvard research. Accessed April 2018 through https://www.inc.com/marissa-levin/the-5- skills-and-behaviors-that-make- entrepreneurs-successful-according-to- harva.html

33. Samuel Markings (2017). Examples of elements without a stable electron configuration. Accessed April 2018 through https://sciencing.com/examples-elements-stable-electron-configuration-36091.html

34. No Name Found: N. No Date Found: s.d. Difference between courage and bravery. Accessed April 2018 through http://www.differencebetween.net/language/difference-between-courage-and-bravery/

35. Melanie Greenburg Ph.D. (2012) The six attributes of courage. Accessed April 2018 through https://www.psychologytoday.com/us/blog/the-mindful-self-express/201208/the-six-attributes-courage

36. Robert Roy Britt (2013) Where did the purple heart from. Accessed April 2018 through https://www.livescience.com/32434-where-did-the-purple-heart-come-from.html

37. Neil Patel (2016) 4 benefits of being an entrepreneur beyond being rich. Accessed May 2018 through https://www.forbes.com/sites/neilpatel/2016/04/18/4-huge-life-benefits-of-being-an-

entrepreneur-being-rich-isnt-one-of-them/#51f641c27fde

38. Greg Uyeno (2016) Mental toll of bad jobs lasts decades. Accessed May 2018 through https://www.livescience.com/55848-job-satisfaction-mental-health.html

39. Neil DeGrasse Tyson (2013). Public twitter post. Accessed March 2018 through https://twitter.com/neiltyson/status/296100559423954944?lang=en

40. No Name Found: N. No Date Found: s.d. Don't write a business plan. Create a lean canvas instead. Accessed March 2018 through https://leanstack.com/leancanvas

41. No Name Found: N. No Date Found: s.d. The Business Model Canvas. Accessed March 2018 through https://strategyzer.com/canvas/business-model-canvas

42. No Name Found: N. No Date Found: s.d. The Value Proposition Canvas. Accessed March 2018 through https://strategyzer.com/canvas/value-proposition-canvas

ACKNOWLEDGMENTS

Anne Williams: Thank you for the constant support, and for your patience when listening to me go on and on about a topic you don't care anything about.

Rod and Kathy Williams: Thank you for raising me to value different points of view, and with the courage to do crazy things like this.

Michael Bromley: Thank you for being the inspiration behind how a focus on key behaviours can lead to a culture of innovation, and for showing me what true leadership is all about.

Jade Firth: Thank you for being an amazing colleague and collaborator, and for the invaluable challenging of ideas that has helped me up my innovation game.

James Morris: Thank you for the many coffee sessions and lunches where we discuss ideas around agility and innovation, and for so openly sharing your in-depth knowledge and experience.

————

Thank you to the content editors for their valuable time, effort and expertise in helping to bring this book and its message to life:

James Morris
Jason Davey
Kyle Williams
Rob Seddon
Taufiq Khan

INDEX

ABOUT THE AUTHOR

Scott Williams is an organisational innovator and operational designer. He leads organisations in the design, adoption and implementation of progressive ways of working based upon lean, design thinking and agile principles that support and drive innovation.

He resides with his family in Sydney, Australia.

www.ingramcontent.com/pod-product-compliance
Lightning Source LLC
Chambersburg PA
CBHW060315220326
41598CB00027B/4332